The Salt Hour

THE
SALT
HOUR

Poems by J. P. White

University of Illinois Press

Urbana and Chicago

© 2001 by the
Board of Trustees of
the University of Illinois
All rights reserved
Manufactured in the
United States of America
♾ This book is printed on
acid-free paper.

Library of Congress
Cataloging-in-Publication Data
White, J. P.
The salt hour :
poems / by J. P. White.
p.   cm.
ISBN 0-252-02636-5 (cloth : alk. paper)
ISBN 0-252-06956-0 (pbk. : alk. paper)
I. Title.
PS3573.H4724S25   2001
811'.54—dc21   00-010698

1 2 3 4 5 C P 5 4 3 2 1

Acknowledgments

Boulevard: "Lady Franklin Writes to Her Husband 15 Years Gone into the Ice"

Crazyhorse: "Arapaima"; "The Drunken Poet Holds Court"; "The Pink Guitar"

Cream City Review: "Elephant Land"

Cumberland Poetry Review: "Breakwall Cats"

Gettysburg Review: "Reading Tu Fu, 1244 Years after He Failed to Secure an Official Scholar's Post"

Green Mountains Review: "After Reading Jeffers's *Original Sin*"; "April at the Mouth of the Russian River"; "The Red Camellia"

Luna: "Red"

Massachusetts Review: "The Bomb"; "The Tree below the Sidewalk Burns"

Memphis State Review: "Barracuda in the Wreck"; "Boy at the Bow of a Sailboat"

New Republic: "Island Vacation"; "What I Said to Him in a Dream as He Eyed the Hanging Beam"

North American Review: "History & Eternity"

One Meadway: "Lobster Boy"

Ontario Review: "Colette's Last Cat"; "Evening with a Hungarian Poet"; "121 Waverly Place"; "Sea Lion"; "Stone Soup"; "To the Black Sailor in Winslow Homer's *Gulf Stream*"

Parnassus: Poetry in Review: "On the Night Train to Nizhni"

Pequod: "The Horse Thief"

Poetry (Chicago): "Living among Women"

Prairie Schooner: "Concerning the Angel at 5th & 53rd"; "On the Guagua at Dawn"; "Russian Daughter"

Sewanee Review: "Apple Trees in the Black Forest"; "The Black Madonna"; "Death of a Ballerina in the Sea of Cortez"; "Erie Squall"; "Family Reunion"; "The Kingfisher"; "The Mole's Dream"; "My Old Sailors on the Graveyard Watch"; "Night Crossing to the Bahamas"; "Three Sisters on Rough Water, 1959"; "Up High in a Bosun Chair"

Shenandoah: "The Effigy of John Donne"

Southern Review: "Essay on Leaves"; "Smoke"

Southwest Review: "On a Day like This"

Tar River Poetry: "Thinking of the Turtle as a Sexual Traveler"

*Water*Stone:* "The Palette of Eternity"

Willow Springs: "Cold Beer"

The author wishes to acknowledge the generous support from the Minnesota State Arts Board and Loft-McKnight Fellowships. Thanks as well to editor George Core for his encouragement over the years and to my indispensable readers: Neil Shepard, Jay Hornbacher, Richard Solly, David Mura, and especially Betty Bright.

For Betty & Vera

Books by J. P. White

In Pursuit of Wings, 1978

The Pomegranate Tree Speaks
from the Dictator's Garden, 1988

What did my father call this life?
One salt hour between two eternities.

Contents

Part 4

PART 1

Boy at the Bow of a Sailboat

> for the pulpit is ever
> this earth's foremost part
> —Herman Melville

Wedged between the pulpit's steel stanchions
I clung one hand to the headstay and conversed,
Hushed or hurried, with the bearded Lord of Breezes.
With the other hand free, I led our sloop
Through sun-knuckled whitecaps as the bow reared
High and shuddered and beat a track to windward.
No one else, I swear, could weather my spray-smacked post,
Not with the lee rail buried and the water hissing past.
Floating, evanescent—my way-showing palm pulsed
Us forward, out over the earth's mother of pearl,
My taut little body splashed and willing
Under the eye of the wind to gaze into the tossed shell
Of the future, look back at my faraway father
Wrapped around the tiller, press close to what falls
And keeps falling from the spark-holding throb of the pulpit.

Three Sisters on Rough Water, 1959

I see it at the last light-clustering wash of sleep,
This black-and-white photo, now gone,
Except for my need to slip it from the sleeve.
On the deck of a sailboat bound for rough water,
There's a boy in the midst of women,
His face lit with the cloudy-green tug of Lake Erie,
One hand grasping the lifeline,
The other on his tilted waist in a defiant show of ballast.
His three older sisters lean over him, as puzzled
By him as he is of their remote, swelling creaturehood.
Their throats touched by medleys stolen from sailors.
Their bodies lingering blue thresholds.
Lipstick shining in the glow of undulating grayness.

The boy can't chart his hungers without dissolving
In the confluence of their moon-shimmered singing,
What do you do with a drunken sailor? What do you do?
He climbs below to curl in the sloop's quarter berth.
White caps rush the length of her keel.
What's a woman, he wonders, as the skipper cries *Hard-a-lee.*
Half asleep, he hears wind opening his sisters' voices
As the *Amorita* rises close to the eye of the wind,
Where the turn happens, the nerves fluttering,
An imperceptible, shuttering kiss of water and sail—
The tack home, so much longer than he remembered.
His three sisters standing watch on the late hours
While he sleeps in the play and service of their beauty.

Lobster Boy

Traveling freak shows brought out the best girls
from the beach. Strange to see them milling

in groups of four or five, picking at wisps
of cotton candy, strolling outside human cages,

wanting in, wanting out, their bronzed bodies,
anonymous and glowing with short breaths

and tiger oil sold in tiny vials for a nickel.
None of the boys believed in mermaids, bearded ladies,

three-hundred-pound witches who crushed men
between their breasts, or hermaphrodites stolen

from the desert. But then we too were afraid
to step behind the glass-bead curtain and deliver

our silence and cobbled laughter. Looking back
on those painfully electric August nights

when the gyrating neons from the Wild Mouse
raced up the dresses of those conspiring girls,

I remember how I was able to hold up the mirror
one night to a boy about my age who was lying

in a shallow tank of salt water at the back of a tent.
My friends had gone to invent their heartache,

and whatever I wanted from a girl would have to wait,
for I had paid my quarter and now I was unable

to take my eyes off the boy's blue shiny skin.
His hands, missing fingers, cupped like pincers.

Legs curved behind his back, the ropy skin
between his feet sewn together forming more of a trunk

than a tail, as was billed on the marquee. Dead
or alive, I couldn't tell, yet the eyes inside

the swollen head flickered—or so I would say later
in a panic. I found a mirror fallen from a purse,

held it beneath his nose. Water bubbled beneath him,
and I ran from the tent, not knowing what I'd seen

or what I felt about his life. I had forgotten
about the blue-skin boy until today when I read

that a blue lobster was found off Maine, a rarity,
seldom trapped, even by the old-timers, thought

a good omen, and actually that's how I've come
to think of that night hovering over that boy

trying to prove him alive in that half-human body
struggling for air or salt or the greater depths

of loneliness beyond the reach of luckless teenagers
who had not yet entered their own curious skins . . .

for though I would spend years believing I must hustle
beautiful girls off the midway to some stretch of beach,

and nearly killed myself with comical, alcoholic plots
when my efforts failed to win the desired sexual twist,

that boy has lingered in the mirror, part of what I am,
small, frightened, curled up, blue with longing

and fear, convinced I'll never know if it's our hunger
that kills or brings life, yet even that question feels

like such a luxury mulled over at a seaside resort,
and some other part of me knows I can never imagine

with what shame and ridicule his pain is jolted
by quarters and mirrors and boys and girls tangled

in their own disguise, escape and hunting quickness,
or out of what oceanic solitude that boy lived, or keeps on

living in a caravan, traveling through the meaning of blue,
broken off from the sun, and the tang of salt air.

Up High in a Bosun Chair

I threaded the wire halyard into the drum
And winched him up the fifty-foot mast.
His bucket of tools dangled from a bosun chair
And nearly always caught at the spreaders
To spook me with its bobbled tipsy climb.
I gripped the winch handle with two fists,
My head throbbing with simple instructions,
My stomach jumping that I might jam a gear,
Lose grip, and send him plummeting to the deck
Of the *Peregrine*. Yet, up there in a breeze,
Above the rooftops, he never seemed to rush
His repairs on a sheave or weather vane.

"How much longer you need?" I shouted up.
"No time at all," his words hung in my ears
Like a riddle plucked out of the sky.
Quiet as a monk, he fiddled with a knife
And pliers with the view of the breakwall,
The water tower, the crisscrossing skiffs,
The bikini girls, maybe even his own death,
All unobstructed for him to look on equally.
While he worked at the top of a sailor's world,
Commenting occasionally on the passing sights,
I gulped thickened air and battled the weight
Of my father's life swinging from my hands.

Erie Squall

In the shade of the swinging boom,
listening to the swell and flap
of sailcloth, I could stretch
my hands out to shore, miles away

and peppered with brightly colored
cottages, touch with my fingertips
the sun-etched clump of trees,
reach far into the heat, ablaze

with pollen and the scent of vineyards
off Catawba, feel the corncob
flicker on its stalk, peel away
the worm coiling among fallen

overripe tomatoes. In that drowsy
reaching, with a bead of sweat
trickling into my eyes, the night
quickened beneath cool Erie glass.

Below that window, perch and pickerel
dropped into infinity, while emerald
waves bubbled upward into whitecaps.
Through the nimbus heat of August

the elements mingled with whoever
I was, mixed with my long-distance eyes,
my pollen-dusted fingers,
and I lay there in the balanced swaying

of a slow-rocking afternoon
until a jolt of wind quivered
across my scalp and the horizon
bruised gray then black,

the waves boiling against the rudder,
my own family failing to outwit
the sky's swollen eye,
our boat pitching under a fury

of fouled lines, heeled over
till we tasted the rusty brass
of that tumbled freighter's lake,
my mother's prayers indistinguishable

from the flashing rain,
my father braced at the helm
shouting commands, the tears shuddering
inside me as my sisters and I

clung to the pulpit, ripped the jib
down the headstay, each of us
peering headlong into the maelstrom
with something akin to joy,

but even this sudden intoxication,
born of cotton clouds,
heat, and an unearthly reaching,
would not last nearly long enough.

Breakwall Cats

The future has its limit, but the past,
What end? Hot sand, green water,
Blue towels, your mother guarding egg-
Salad sandwiches, eyeing her daughters.
There they are, your aunt and uncle
Digging at one another's troubles
As though picking fleas from a stray.
Those strange, blood-filled freckles
On your uncle's belly swimming in oil.
Your cousin in her leopard bikini, full
Of travels with her stunt man from Bolinas,
Her legs as long as the word *pickerel*.

Your three sisters envious of her Italian,
Her sleek body coiled beneath an arm
Of driftwood. Your father, off by himself,
Bundling the spinnaker on the lawn.
When the wind kicks up, you will all go
Sailing, ride the pull of the rudder
Flinging spray in your faces. No one
Has divorced yet or wandered off or suffered
From chronic pain or drinking. No one
Knows who will light the little explosions
Or never ship back from Rio after holiday.
Penny-rich, undivided in your affections,

The waves never collapse as night floods in.
Everyone's still in motion—the unfooled
Shuffleboard masters, the giant canasta queens,
The scrubbed, shining, unavailable girls—
All swept beneath the lighthouse swiveling
Its head like an owl. After stars flicker,
You slip down to the jagged, seaweed breakwall
Where men with lanterns and black whiskers
Fish for bass and sheepshead—while cats,
Thin and exhausted from sickness, lean
Between rocks and bait cans, skittish, shadowy,
Hissing from hiding places few have ever seen.

Family Reunion

After decades apart, they sail again on green water.
Of the lake, it is bright with islands, bays, and cuts.
The promise of wind stands before them blessing.
They eat with the appetite of pirates thrilled by the glint
Of doubloons in the deep cold sweeping outward.
Their bodies gimbal with the slow rocking of the hull
And remember the path of waves shaping valleys.

To the north, dark sooty clouds gather and bear down.
Gusts fray ripples into white threads crossing.
Rain breaks the land and locks down their seeing.
As the darkness gains, a glow outlines their faces.
It's the flint of storms long past and electrical
When they danced on the deck of their youth
And wrote their best stories with the sky leaping.

All over the lake, boats douse their sails in a flurry,
Motor back to port under bare poles nodding.
They watch the blue-black storm swinging lower
And know it will reach them in a lunge of running.
They drop the jib, reef the mainsail, press on.
They expect the bang and snap of the storm's descent,
But ice? They didn't count on hail the size of quarters.

The father leans against the combing, popping stones
In his mouth like maraschino cherries. He is cold
To the elbows and smiling. The mother sits below,
No longer thunder-trapped with steepled hands aching.
She too winks at the roar of the ice and twisted rain.
One sister sprawls on the foredeck, nose into the light
And dark dissolving. She sees in the family the color

Of slate-blue sparks weaving across broken water,
Holding them to the long sheaves of summer ice
As they breathe fire into each other's wet faces
And laugh. She hoists her arms like lightning rods,
Not to signal down death, but to keep her family shining
In the midst of darkness on board their little boat—
Their ark, their crown of spray plumes falling,

Their spitfire bite of sail thinning as it fills.

Night Crossing to the Bahamas

The choir sang of the beautiful city, the walls
Of sapphire and amethyst, the new tabernacle lit
Behind twelve pearls, Alpha-Omega, pain shall be no more.

But who could wait that long, the boy thought, as the wind
Kicked at the thin church doors, and he heard the waves
Rolling up the beachhead like barrels off a plank.

Every woman in a robe was going away, candlestick by pew,
Back to paradise, but at midnight he was shipping out
With his father to sail past paradise across the Stream.

There they would find all the wind of the world harnessed
To their sails and the boy would lean over the toerail,
See beneath the rooms of phosphorescence, the anchors

Of sunken ships, bottles with sealed messages, the swirling
Hair of Medusa, all the mirrors of his childhood
He feared to look into, with death hidden from view.

He would dip his hands in the sibilant foam falling
From the bow, hold the beautiful city, all the bronze doors,
Domes and arches speckled with a bluish-green patina,

The avenues and lattice-covered gardens alive with sparks
And the shimmer of newly minted coins dropped in fountains.
There he would shuffle with island women swaying

On thin balconies in brightly colored silks and earrings.
And just beyond reach in the coral depths, he would glimpse
The great cathedral, the streets of gold, the book of the Lamb,

The angels, the martyrs, then near dawn, it would all start
To fade, flickering somewhere below their sleek ocean craft
Whose rudder left a wake that seemed wide enough to follow.

Barracuda in the Wreck

Twenty feet down, kicking hard,
I fight back cramps, my body swirling
On one breath around rotted bulkheads,
Gaping holes, prowling blown hatches
For the listless grouper stroking its pocket of eternity.

Below the wreck's waterline,
Beneath algae hanging like spaghetti,
Where the transom cracks,
There I spot my prize,
A ten-pound lunker lulled in weeds,

Swaying back in shadowed cavity.
I load the spear
With thick black bands of the sling,
Take aim below its eyes,
Pierce my fish through the pectorals.

It shudders out of hiding, flails,
Skips to shake loose.
I drive the flared barbs through torn speckled scales.
I relax my grip as the grouper thuds against
Metal, turn to rise with my breath

Swelling chest and head.
Dogging my periphery,
A barracuda swings like a hull of silver,
Its eyes glowing amethyst,
An irradiated light,

An ember throbbing around me
As the pressure builds at the temples,
Ribs flickering,
Every muscle tightening, the air whining
In my throat when the barracuda lights out

From its anchor of hallucination,
Hits the end of my spear.
I look down to see the shaft
Spiraling into the ink of the wreck,
The giant grouper gone, dark bubbles

Spinning from my clenched teeth,
Wristbones stung with the pass of death,
But not dead, nothing from a Bahamian patch
Of blue to feed memory but thunder in the ears,
A tight cartwheel of blood,

The sweet gasp of air, the light that kills from below.

PART 2

Colette's Last Cat

On an evening in June when bumblebees were still swinging
on the pendulous white orb of peonies, and I'd nearly forgotten
about the chronic muscle spasms shooting across my shoulders,
I saw the giant green parrot sitting on the ridge of my neighbor's
    roof
and my striped cat palpitating on the window ledge, her tail
    swelling,
her heart breaking, certain that her most exotic, maddening
    interlude
had finally arrived. I wanted to capture the parrot, for out of its
    cage
in Minnesota, it could not last but a few nights on tight-clipped
    wings,
but I didn't know its name or how to climb high the worn
    shingles.
Instead, I watched *Tigre* crouched low, eyes glistening tangerine
and vermilion, and I thought of Colette, and how she saw
    herself,
toward the end, as the last Parisian cat, arthritic and curled up
like a turban beside an open window, still fickle and searching
the alleys of her arrondissement for the object of greatest
    curiosity,
her upper ledge emptied for the coming badinage, gambling
    years
of looking for the privilege of one more assignation with the
    laugh
of a passing child or the sudden twirl of a parasol, because even
    it,
her precious, hated, irreconcilable pain, fed on isolation and
    complaint,

even it would one day, soon enough, vanish to play with
        someone else,
just as, in a freshening breeze, the parrot flew off over the oaks,
and my cat, exhausted by the sudden removal of the perfect,
        painful
aphrodisiac, flopped over to dream again of a salacious variety
of traps, any colossal moments of astonishment and unscalable
        myth.

Two Mosquitoes in the Blue Smoke Light

See them there
wrapped inside translucent amber,
fifty million years ago

when the sap-running conifers
flypaper-trapped them,
then crashed to the sea floor,

transporting these two lovers
in flight to some mummied
undertow of steamed volcanic water.

Death or rejuvenation?
Who can say what love endures?
Inside this airtight, watertight boat

of gold shaped like a human thumb,
they tumble through bubbled debris,
wearing blue smoke light

on their wings, their bodies
diaphanous and agitated
from the original heave of fire

and still coupling in slow motion—
the first monsters flung into coals,
the first angels risen from mottled creation.

Red

The color of warning for ships,
lobsters tucked beneath ledges,
and the all-breathing mangrove root.
Flameleaf, frostfire—the woods
struck by the seven gold candlesticks
of Revelation walking at dusk.
The red of rubies, cutthroat trout,
and the coat you put on at the end
of the river released into the sea.
The color of change found
in flags, wine, poppies,
barbiturates. In most places,
a color used sparingly,
but not on this island of the machete
swung from the waist by boys
who know the bright splash
of pig's blood on their hands
before they learn to read.
Their father wears a smeared apron.
Their gutted pig hangs from its hind feet.
A thin-ribbed white dog drinks
from a pool swelling below the animal.
They started before first light
to take the creature down into death.
A snarl of flies has found
the soft mortal eyes. Tonight,
the family will feast on red pork
dressed in red mango chutney.
The sun will drape into the sea

like a necklace of lava beads.
The beer will flow. The boys will laugh.
The ancient charcoal heat
of their eating will bring
everything red back to life.

The Mole's Dream

Fortressed here
in the earth's dim tunnel
under weight of centuries
and today's wet leaves,
it takes so long
for these spadelike hands
to paddle through a cluster
of bulb-rot roses
to the solitary worm.
Hunger's reward:
A stubborn pink nose
that shoves against
the whole earth,
winning only few
of the sweetest grubs.
All this travel
twisting over cracks,
ledges, stones, spidery roots
gone hideous with age
is a lonely trudge without stars.
Vision! Vision!
That's what these mole eyes want,
and small swallow wings
to fit perfectly this husk
crouched under thumping rain.
Imagine, brief life,
the silken thread of flight,
all-seeing, all-knowing,
rising over the world's rim
on a sudden swerve

around the jutting shoulder
of the next mountain.
No more jagged rockface
to thread with passageways.
Only plenty of light to steer by,
and the company of sky.

The Horse Thief

After years of bone cracking, acupuncture, deep massage,
physical therapy, ultrasound, trigger-point injections,
painkillers, and a spiritual healer named Wendylee Rose

Hummingbird, who said I'd been a horse thief in a past life
and was hanged one morning near a river in South Dakota,
I thought every doctor and holistic health expert

needed an ego manipulation and some chronic charley-horse
muscle spasm to put their practice into perspective.
"Lighten up," everyone said, but I couldn't turn my neck

left or right, let alone up, after the first misfit chiro,
trying to fix my headaches, strapped me into a medieval
traction device, flipped the switch, and watched me buck

on a table like a tinhorn tossed on the back of a brahma bull.
Quacks, quasi-quacks, criminal quacks, and quack-quacks—
that's how I'd come to rate the certified and uncertified

healers who dabbled in neck, back, and shoulder complaints.
As I imagined the noose cinched around my Adam's apple
one morning in South Dakota, I thought of Uncle Bryce,

the osteopath, who snapped backs into place in exchange
for a few prime fishing hours on private ponds stocked
with smallmouth bass. Patients from all over Ohio,

including my father, who couldn't find relief anywhere else,
turned up in his waiting room. To fix a lower back,
he'd flick an ankle. To treat a neck, he'd knead

the lower trapezius. Just when you were relaxed, thinking
about where he snagged the trophy muskie, he'd jerk you
into place, some broken part of yourself suddenly mended.

Years later, after my parents moved far from Ohio,
I found him in a nursing home for distant, nodding men
waving to fishing boats on the muddy Vermilion River.

Scrunched up in a cot, he mumbled about his wife,
a woman he loved only as far as duty allowed,
and a first son who flew his Blue Angel into a mountain—

a slow unappeasable sadness tilting his legs
in different directions as he talked. One night,
after treating a patient, the house of his body

flashed over. A stroke shut down his brain. His legs
sizzled beneath like cut wires. All the sleuthing
touch of his hands was gone, along with the winding in

of the Shakespeare and Garcia reels. Yet he fought back
from the dead by reaching over to Danny Pasavitch,
the former high school fullback, who lived across the hall

with his hands permanently clenched into fists.
As neighbors they worked out a code, scrawling inside
each other's hands. No man in our family could hold Bryce

as he was, withered to a stretch of skin, so Bryce
rocked Danny in his arms as the boats with their cargo
of perch and pickerel slid by the breakwall toward the icehouse.

After Danny twisted off to sleep, Bryce chattered
to anyone who would listen about sweet jesus throwing out
the eye's great treasures until the spirit broke

into a single unstoppable beam surrounding the brother.
Leaning over my uncle that day stroking his temples,
I kept hoping I could help him exhale his life's ashes,

until his chest, his throat, his mouth opened
and let fall one syllable for the bass ponds we fished
on Wednesday afternoons behind cattails, alone with
          dragonflies,

lily pads, frogs, and the electric expectation of something
rising from the dark of the pond to change our luck.
Today, still angry with myself and with my father,

your only brother, for not coming to your funeral
because a blizzard blew in off Lake Erie, I wanted to talk
with you about my neck, which sounds like one of those

gravel fishing roads we traveled down in your Studebaker.
But even more than my aching neck bones, I wanted
to ask you about the spirit, if through its embrace

the edges of the future blurred without fear,
and if the past could be reentered and changed?
Together, with what you had learned before you left

the earth in a snowstorm, I thought, for a moment,
we could go back to that miserable third-down play
when Danny was hooked from behind by a nose tackle.

With your hands once again working out the knots wrenched
under the skin, every weak and frightened memory flaming
in Danny's body, and my own, and my father's and yours,

could be found and extinguished, all the way back
to that windless morning beside a river in South Dakota
when a man was hoisted up into a tree and hanged by his neck

for stealing horses, even that man, unknown to all of us,
even he could be brought back to earth where your spirit
might brush along his neck like a zephyr that had traveled

a long way in an instant and in an instant was gone.

Kingfisher

Standing out there, waist deep in the Clarks Fork River,
straightening out my line, thirty feet of it, and landing
a dry fly inches from a cutthroat climbing unhurried morning
    light,
I could almost taste the pine-needle green of the time before
    time
was strapped on a wrist and divided into boredom, exactitude,
worry, acceleration. I didn't care if my legs were numb

from the rush of bright glacial water or about the Royal
    Coachman
I lost on a sunken log. Everywhere I looked I saw tanagers
darting the roof of that world like banana-yellow canaries
shaken loose from a cage. One eagle threaded river loops
and vanished in the gorge above a waterfall. Where I anchored
my boots in current, the sweep of flat water between rapids

bubbled with unsuspecting fingerlings, spurred the kingfishers
from their perches. I had heard their loud dry rattle, their cranky
throatiness made to match the bushy, punker hairdo, but I'd
    never seen
such revved-up wackiness, their staggered, downshifting wing
    beats
timed for the perfect plunge, the trout wedged in the big, dark
    bill,
then up they raced to a festive breakfast nook glazed by sun.

For that hour when the hatch was on and my arm became the
        bend
in the river, I saw those ragged solitary birds as the very essence
of the tale, the true measure of our worth, the oldest Fisher
        Kings
swooping between past and future like blue-stained meteoric
        stones.
And why shouldn't I give them a divine, incomprehensible
        status?
Up river at Cooke City, news comes of gold, the old claims

snatched up by big Canadian wallets. The memory of a single
pickaxe blow and gargantuan nuggets has busted a road to Cody
for the trucks, the workers, and the slow stream of mobile
        homes, trailers,
and satellite dishes. The inevitable leaching of the cyanide vats,
standing at the headwaters, is the subject of only occasional
        roadside
wrangling, the next crushed beer can. But for the clownish
        kingfisher

hovering on rapidly beating wings, practiced in the art of
        freewheeling
insouciance, you can see the Clarks Fork is more pleasing than
        gold,
horses, hides, talc, wheat, dried meat, butter, cheese. It's the
        white
ribbon wrapped around the grail, the source of aerial boldness,
        strength,
renewal, the place where play breaks down fortune and cold
        clear water
reveals quick, flashing, prodigal fish once prized above all else.

Arapaima

"The world's largest freshwater fish, found
in the Amazon basin, nicknamed 'water monkey'"

Her underwater microphoned breathing
pulses louder than her voice
naming the endangered species
of the Caribbean coral reef—

its purples, yellows, reds lit
with her rushed coagulated bubbles.
The more amplified her oxygen count
the more I sink in my own air

among the yelping, disconnected children
pressed against the aquarium.
I'm the only giant here
weighted with my claims on the future,

wanting every striped gilled swimmer,
even the ones with military names,
to nibble from the hand of a protector
in the midst of an emerald swirl.

I reel from the diver's feeding show,
hurry past the zigzag children
and the row of electric eels
back to a thickly brambled tank,

second home of the sleek arapaima,
spewed from the choked banks
of the smoky Amazon basin
stranded below the equator—

its mouth believed by river tribes
to unhinge at night
when it climbs twisted branch limbs
for rodents, parakeets, bats.

Vanilla orchid, heart of palm, rosewood,
and so much oxygen laboring
out of the lungs of a rain forest.
Beneath those dizzy vulnerable trees

standing like clumps of vegetables,
I picture the earth's muddy river veins
spidering toward the Atlantic
over tailing dunes and buzzed eucalyptus.

A ventilating fish roots along the floor.
Watching it hang in milky light,
I wanted to mourn the burning air
and this big-eyed armored ghostfish

denied its channel of transfiguration—
when it stirs from leathery scales,
breaks tunnel, leaps out of mud,
a water monkey howling from the vines.

The diver's pail of squid swings
empty from her wrist. She climbs
her umbilical cord back to the surface.
The sergeants major settle below the fans.

Sea Lion

Only the largest ocean wave can drive him from the ledge.
For three months he cannot leave his harem even for food.

Such vigil requires fat and brooding and power.
Much of his work today demands keeping his eight wives

from slipping away in search of skate and squid
and the small sharks he can catch in one corkscrew tour

of the sea floor. And what about his roar inside the cave?
It spirals through the vault and looming headland,

diminishes the slosh and boom of the waves against walls.
All this bellowing to fend off the rogue bachelor bulls

who seek possession of the breeding herd. Our guide says
females show no loyalty, and when a harem breaks down

by storm, the bull may never recover his chosen mates.
Loss of weight. Exhaustion. Solitude. Puffery—

the ancient cost of maintaining a throne. Yet when
he lifts up his chest in a tight curl and delivers

his pronouncements to the scampering wives below,
we tremble and scramble back up the cliff. Hear it?

The steep and wild Oregon cape carries the grotto roar.
It is a male sound from below—delirious, proud,

uncompromising, undissolved, and as old as the floating
igneous basalt. Hear it? What can we do now, but listen?

One Tory Tells the Story of the
Red-Tufted Crane's Return

April is flooded with birds teasing out
Their mating songs. Don't you find their melodies
Acceptable? You're not the first to tout
The heady island perfumes. No, I've never

Clipped a weed. My wife calls these hedges
Her illuminated Bible. Did I tell you our estate was part
Of Henry VIII's private hunting grounds? The sedge
And trees are centuries old, dearly protected.

That's how we like Sutton-Surrey, filled
With families of pedigree. Still, this near London,
Riffraff caper at Empson Downs, squirreled
Behind the track. At night, as a boy, I'd creep there

Looking for Juicy Fruit from Yankee boys.
I'd watch them in their tents with flashlights,
Jerking over girlie mags. You Americans toy
With young birds more than us. When I was ten

I saw the first torn circles of smoke, Luftwaffe
Skidding bombs on Croydon. Churchill, all he had
Was bluff and wooden rifles. See this specimen.
It's a bullet pried loose from my schoolyard wall.

Don't talk about German Reunification. All wars
Are started by Slavic-German scum, little men
Tinkering in basements, sewing up boot scars.
After the last bombs, Labor broke our backs,

Along with Unionists and Third World blight,
One and the same. If Wilson hadn't made concessions,
Britain would still be Britain. Yes, the blue and white
Is Ming. The ivory dragon is from Singapore.

Would you care to sip courvoisier? Don't get me
Started on that tunnel with the Frogs. Can't stand
The lot, even if they do serve the best recipes
For our Dover sole. French, Italians everywhere.

I hate dashing to their restaurants, but it's agreed
We've never learned to stir a sauce. I don't mind
Some foreigners as long as they're not Pakistani,
Who've taken over our tube and ambulance service.

Some squabbling in the corn is probably good, gears
The organism to spawn antibodies. Take the crane.
It's been missing from our island some 400 years.
Just today I read it's returning from Asia or Egypt

To nest in the outer marshes. How did one vignette
Describe the bird (once the favorite quarry
In falconry and served at Henry's royal banquets)?
The ungainly, striped, tufted, red-crowned crane.

Stone Soup

The wind cuts through my clothes when we walk.
She wears a thin black leather jacket. No hat. No gloves.
She works two jobs. Six days a week.
How do you make stone soup taste better?
You throw in more stones.
It's a little joke from this little Russian woman
Whose son was born with an incurable heart
The same year her husband died before he was forty.
She had no money for operations.
She taught the boy to swim against the current
Of a cold river after working in the hot sun
Digging carrots and potatoes. He was three.
She told him he would grow *strong as a lion*
By slipping down into the dark and bitter.

No one loves the thieves hung beside Christ
More than the Russians. What is broken
Will be fed garlic, cayenne, vinegar.
Punishment will come from not reaching out
To touch the hem of the invisible.
Can't you see him? The boy dog-paddling
Back and forth through algae and moss,
The chill pumping up through the roots of the river
To blast blood into his chest, then as he settles
Into his shivering she drags him into the sun
And points him back for more ice plunges.
Seven times they do this each summer day
For seven years until the boy is a man,
His unstoppable, stolen heart flushed with fire

and a knowledge of rivers cold enough for lions.

Elephant Land

Propped in a low-slung chair,
watching the easy sway of families
bending to their games and oils,
you could live in this Florida beach town.
Yet out there in the blue, blue-green,
past the indigo shallows and the circling plane
trailing a block-lettered advertisement,
the Gulf Stream churns and tears north
to Newfoundland. A father tells his son,
who is busy building a crab-shelled fort,
"That's elephant land out there, see them
throwing spray with their trunks?"
The boy glances at the thick-slanting ridges,
returns to his architectural curio taking shape
in a delicate sand ledge.   The Gulf is a charge
of giant blue elephants sweeping thunder.
Only weeks ago a ship lost headway there,
capsized under crags while still in sight.
No "Mayday" rang out over radio, no flash
skipped from the navigator's mirror. Not a soul
washed in with the surf. Nothing, not even a shoe,
was found the next day in the swirling caverns
bright as church windows. The father turns
from the tight-running shoulders, eager to leave
this scene of repose, when the boy shouts,
"I see them, I see the elephants." He throws down
his Clorox-bottle shovel, points with both hands
to the darkest blue water rippling higher than a house
on the horizon: "When can we go to elephant land?"

Thinking of the Turtle as a Sexual Traveler

You slept through geckoes
Flipping the little switch inside their ballooning throats.
I woke thinking of the woman we'd met at the black sand beach.
How broad and strong her shoulders.
How much older and wrinkled she was than us,
Beat by rain and a rainbowed sun, after her trips
Across Sudan and South America.
Now, she bicycle rode solo around the Big Island volcanoes.
I admit I found her attractive,
Drawn to her unspoken decision
To trade cleverness for astonishment.
I offered her snorkel gear to watch
Speckled hawksbills flying beneath waves,
Their long flattened limbs like wings skimming air.
She swam out much farther than I expected,
Past the seawall lagoon to the second row of coral reefs.
She kicked deep into rough white seas.
I glimpsed her head bobbing among turtles sipping air.
"She's not coming back," I remember telling you.
The earth's oldest hand pulled her back, pushed her forward,
Scissored her legs above blossoming mounds of coral.
Her downward gaze sustained by mossy turtles
Spinning their unhurried feeding through beams
Of green sea-filtered sunlight.
How much stored turtle memory floated with her from
        millenniums past,
The migrations of fish, wind shifts, ocean currents,
Volcanic eruptions, tropical flower perfumes.
What the water tears down, the fire builds.
As the flapping turtles turned inside their hard, heavy shells,
She drifted at the gleam's edge,

So much a part of the outer reef I fell asleep
Beneath palms and forgot about her swimming with turtles.
Our breathing echoed the lapping of her waters.
Air softened around us in wet folds.
The tradewinds stirred up
Hints of sea grape, barnacled wood, ginger.

Death of a Ballerina in the Sea of Cortez

Where the Pacific kisses
The Sea of Cortez and stirs up
Old ocean plumes of fire and mullet blood,
The big sails feed, run, and die for sport.
Before they do, they dance.
Which is how you might like
To sign your deal with death.
No babbling, incontinence, pills, disease.
Just one last aerial pirouette.
The ten-footer I saw die
Vaulted its body length above water.
Its dorsal fin billowed like a spinnaker
Violet in the morning sun.
Suspended, painted navy blue on air,
It tailwalked its 150 pounds,
Stitching bill and silver belly to sea and sky—
As you might like to claim you did
Before thrashing onto the curl of the gaff.
To stand or walk on only air
Would be a final stunt, a fitting resurrection.
But to sky high enough to abandon
The weight of all that held you under,
To fall back, submarine, gain speed, bullet
Out of the depths, break the crush of foam,
To twist, swivel, summon all
To shake loose from the hook
And dance at the reel-screaming end,
Brawling with god, man, and the velvet-smooth
Sea you were born to—that would be a death
You might hold out for just to see
If you could blend, in one acrobatic maneuver,

The flying up with the forever crashing down.
But it will never happen that way.
The man who kills the sail
Kills the dance before he dies.
For in his love of the ballerina's last leap,
He sees only himself, lovely and large,
Dancing on the Sea of Cortez,
Only himself, filling out the fighting chair,
A hero, a winner, a sport,
One of the lucky ones granted a channel
To run deep, rise, live on.

PART 3

Sugar

The jimjam government man lingers near strapless tops
Of blonde German women, scoffs at the local rum,
And orders English gin. *Trading up*, he says, looking
Down to the harbor where the stark island lights

Undulate like a waist of stars. He carries a spider streak
Of talcum powder beneath his eyes' umber pockets.
Every night he buys back a little more whiteness
By selling thin mahogany girls to darker men.

It's prime business, he adds, winking me over to a honey
In a cream cotton blouse. Her breasts swing like stones
Found loose in the silky caves of avocados.
Peel me, her eyes say, *peel lick swallow*.

If it's sweet, you can taste the bitter, a Jamaican says,
Leaning into me. He tells how the Brits built
Empire one teaspoon at a time. How biscuits and jam
Gave ballast to the long-raked timbers racing water.

I keep looking at her looking at me, thinking
Marmalade, preserves, condensed milk, sherbet.
Her skin a sheet of gold chocolate to scratch,
But when I scan the teeth of the man who works her,

I see the crosses of that day's mountain road—bleached,
Leaning at fallen angles in grass. Salt air had eaten
The grave names. The beach below through palms
Scribbled like a chalk line or a spilled cup of sugar.

One boy cast a net into surf. The scene passed without a lens
To click it, yet returns through the crease of his smile.
I know then the night bears down like a reef stoked
With rusted keel bolts. Everywhere the cost of whiteness

Jacks up the ball and chain of a hiploose island music.
Nothing will be sold that hasn't been savored before:
The soft angles, the fingertip pull of cloth, the quick
Unbuttoning, the jibs whipping through a sea of cane.

On the Guagua at Dawn

We slept in five-dollar hotels, listening to waves slap blue paint
On hot white sand. So many watery portraits to choose from.
How shall we rise and dissolve today? I waited out boat repairs,
A change of crew, weather. You, the color of molasses bubbled
    up
From boilers, waited for another life to grip you tight as a bottle.
Death was not on the menu as the tongue traveled wet salt skin.
I'm not saying I want to go back to the blur between lassitude
    and dancing,
Unless I could find again that guagua we boarded, jammed with
    women
Bound for market, their baskets swollen with mangoes, lemons,
Breadfruit, yams, roosters, piglets. I sat crowded out by thighs
    and laughter
And the watchful hat brims of old men. While the palm-leaf
    mountains
Sailed by our window, I held on to that ride as the true life, the
    real one,
Always before just out of reach and belonging to someone else:
The first light streaming into sloping cane, the dragonflies
    hovering
Like emeralds and rubies, then spilling into sinuous troughs of
    dust.
The kingdom almost entered at daybreak. The bus rocking us
    there.

Island Vacation

Her lips the color of smeared pomegranate seeds.
His Adam's apple raw as the head of a spike.
Her voice like water spilling over a reef.
His voice slow and accusing like a ring of smoke.

She orders grouper with lime butter and hazelnuts.
He settles for shrimp with star anise and orange.
He has always leaned on the power of her praise.
She has always feared his censure and depression.

The waves run out like the scratching of a pen.
In an alphabet whisper, she hears the writing
And the unwriting of their story like a tremor
Of how the island rose out of molten ash.

Tomorrow they will tilt the beach umbrella.
They will marvel at the topless German beauties.
They will see couples who've risen exhausted
From crumpled bed sheets, eager to return.

She will watch a sweat bee burrow in the sand.
He will eye a woman dressed for a sex scene.
Before their world falters he will plot his escape.
She will hear again the hours of their diminishment.

She will wonder what their moment is missing.
He will think he still looks decent at fifty-five.
This is the permanent sadness of island vacations:
Two people travel a great distance to watch

The blazing sunlight turn their shadows black.
They want to return to old familiar pleasures.
Yet by the time they arrive in paradise, they speak
In anger or not at all and they never enter the water,

Which stays warm enough to soothe and cradle.

The Pink Guitar

Once in Nicaragua I saw a pink guitar.
The man who played it wore a straw hat,
The color of his cigarette-stained gold fillings.
He'd been a soldier in the war. He fought
Against everyone, he said. No one understood
His land. The jungle swallowed his melodies.

He'd cut his farm out of leaves the size of horses.
The rains broke his road into pieces of bruised
And sagging fruit. His ankles looked
Like they'd been fished out of sinkholes.
He'd just sold the last of his coffee beans and corn.
The tip of his tongue swiveled at the corner

Of his mouth like a chameleon's tail.
The fretboard of his pink guitar
Was made of yellow laurel wood.
He'd given his life to Christ since the war.
In his face, a pain rooted in a forgotten pleasure.
He wore the rain like a second set of clothes.

While a boy sharpened a blood-stained machete
On a leather strap, the man played pink songs
In between long blended swells of mountain green.
His music was not poor and dispossessed.
It was surrounded by rivers running
The ragged curve between birth and death.

Once in Nicaragua I saw a pink guitar.

Concerning the Angel at 5th & 53rd

Every city has them—pools of helmeted, stained men
Clustered around engines grinding through night.
White arc lights sear the jagged, scraped surface
Of dirt and cut stone as the men stand guard
Over broken water mains, busted sewer lines, road repair.
Who knows how long they've been there, caught
By the old mephitic street vapors, swallowed by the noise
Of machinery, the long blue flashes of smoke?
Where much is lacking, faces say, there are many wishes.
Or so it seemed after midnight at 5th and 53rd
When this black woman in tight red shorts, lacy blouse,
And black bra clipped past men cutting out a section
Of curb with backhoe and jackhammers.
                                        A riveting Giotto
Angel, she'd plunged to earth to fill momentarily the wing
Of a triptych. As she turned the corner, a white man hunched
Over a hammer, took his eyes off his work, "Hey, Valentine,
I'll take some of that." With his compressor hissing over
Taxi horns, she never noticed his pain when the hammer
Hit his boot, probably broke his foot. He slumped, wailing,
Ripped the gold cross from his neck as though he might
Heave it after her. I could see in his eyes how close
Hate is to love—the Angel of Mercy now an ugly cunning
Fury, the source of so much uninhaled pollen, the cause
Of the world cut in twain—as she vanished deep into
The luminous fibers of the next block, both answering
And failing to answer the many prayers she had heard.

History & Eternity

At that moment when the nose of the DC-9 breaks
over clouds, curled like blown-white hurricane spume,

yet also arranged quietly like roses, the city stalls
beneath rain, returns to its cabs wedged between trucks,

the half-torn umbrellas, the porn shops glittering
ALL TEEN GIRLS. At that point of acceleration,

I can hear my Christian Science Sunday school teacher
saying death is like a handshake, a bridge, the No

that becomes the Yes, part of our wide human orbit,
and I see myself strapped into the cone of a spacecraft,

ready to shake the glove of the unforeseen, like now,
except for my persistent memory of this jazzman

bopping into the Avenue of the Americas, barefoot,
clownish, confused by so much speeding chrome.

I'm yelling, "Get the hell out of there," but he can't
hear me or anyone else before *smack*, he's clipped

from behind by the hood of a tinted limo. Then,
the traffic snarl, the sirens, everyone honking

at this man who died in the street where death must be
pale and downward and unavailable to a crossing.

I pushed closer to give a statement, my teacher's phrase,
called home tangled in my head with *blindsided,*

but the police waved me off as I neared the stretcher.
I wanted to tell them I saw this pink carnation,

eternal almost in the clumsy flight of its petals,
bursting bright and weightless from his buttonhole.

What I Said to Him in a Dream as
He Eyed the Hanging Beam

What about that fissure Rilke speaks of
Between the exact ending
Of a year and the beginning of the next,
When the cold snaps off the hands of clocks
And you enter the joinery of hours,
The corners of your breathing. The edges. The truth.
I'll help you stop the stars from reeling.
Together, we'll study the microscopic tear in the calendar.
See where the harm has been done by you and by others.
Most men refuse to open the lower, jammed drawer
Of their own story, to finger the Rosetta stone.
But not you.
You're ready for the glare of hieroglyphics,
What you wrote, in fear or anger, to some part of yourself.
To desire death won't give you or me
Enough love to last the night.
And then, who knows,
We may still have to travel the earth in search of lost pages.
I need your weakness, its weight,
Your relics found at the back of a museum,
Telling you, as a man,
You've failed to deliver the rope of gold.
Wherever you go with your grief,
Remember any keyhole contains constellations.
No matter how you scribe the arc of lost power,
You're more than a man shoved into the sleeves of a heavy coat.
More than a stack of scribbled ink.
You're my new world cloud, motionless, monumental,
Floating above the worn, damp, marble statues,

And broken steps where you take yourself back to the beginning
When all this pain and mischief began.
In your true form,
You can slip through any aperture.
You can see. You can see and read the sealed envelopes.

April at the Mouth of the Russian River

Everything comes to birth and death, including April.

At Goat Rock Beach, shy harbor seals
Deliver their pod of milking pups.
They nudge sunward on hind flippers like caterpillars.
Nearby, a dead seal rocks on the sand like a bloated spruce.
It's a bright collision,
This crossing of ends and beginnings,
The shine of friction making this place
Green and voluptuous and our story, brief.
We leave behind the crush of abalone,
Climb past bay and sage,
Thinking how a child of ours might run here.
Up behind thinning redwoods, we lie down on raincoats.
We talk through wind of the coming adoption.
Our voices reach toward the *taiga* of another Russia.
An orphanage there, a girl, who will take our names.
What we bring close, cracks us open to greater distance:
All these journeys outward curved with desire,
The loneliness of desire,
And the looping talon shadows of the red-tailed hawk.
The sound of water expands and contracts
Inside the gold field our bodies share with the first gnats
    humming.
After love, we worry about mountain lions.
Will the tracks we saw find us without clothes?
As if laughing at our fear,
Gold-crowned sparrows roll in the dust, splashing,
This is good, this will do, there's no end to April fools.
Back at the breakwall,

A new, inescapable violence blooms in the fat.
The whiskered pups slip away from the slurp of milk.
They make ready for their first sweep
Into the ground-swell mouth
That takes and takes with no regard for the quiver of infants.

Smoke

With first snow, I think of first fire,
the earth wrapped by flame and ash
and swept by waves of running darkness.

Tonight, no less cruel and sanguine.
The sky's steel edge softened by pearls.
Chimney smoke chugs each house

into the safety of a terminal warmth
and the crackle of pine sap
speeding tinder stud walls.

Each room an engine for breath
and the curving horizon any life makes.
If we are frail columns of smoke

as the psalmist claims, how explain
the weight of this snow and our tracks
through it glimpsed from an upper window,

so many places to go and no end
to the cold and the fire holding together
the pillars of this restless planet.

It is a lovers' despair and this poem's,
to fashion an imperishable love
from bodies that perish, to travel so far

to arrive at this house only to one day
let the years vanish like smoke
curling up from a burning page,

no telling how the last day
will be born in us, through what veil
we will say we saw a flicker

of whiteness coming down or rising.

The Tree below the Sidewalk Burns

"A conversation about trees is almost a crime."
—Bertolt Brecht

The postmoderns have it all wrong. Meanings find us.
Signposts and symbols lay scattered over the earth.
Their random colors and shapes destined to coalesce.
Remember the last scene in that play about fire
When the father takes the match to the bucolic postcard
Hand-painted by Hitler, lets go, through ignition,
Of the jagged memories he's used to define his life.
Lets go long enough to walk out into the snow
With his landscape-architect son he's never loved.
The father's memory of fire replaced with a smaller fire
That frees. In the turning of an apartment doorknob,
The historical lineaments are suspended. The air clears.
We saw the father's body strengthen its relationship
To the vertical, both the downward weight of his feet
And the upward alignment of his head and shoulders.

A new breath flushed his lungs, drawn from the postcard's
Blue-black flame, the sting of cold, and the clatter
Of wooden shoes on cobblestones as SS guards drove
Families out of boxcars to the camps. It was a breath
Mixed with history but not condemned to it. Afterward,
Near our hotel, we saw the tree living below the grate
In a sea of butts and trash, still green, breathing, on fire,
Pushing skyward, impossibly rising through steam, glass,
Scraps of food, rancid flowers. This tree reminded us
Of that father walking the snow—tenacious, unavailable,
Caged, aloof, liberated, a Jew ready to send signals,
Not always of hope and wind in the branches, but then

He was the last survivor in his family and his children
Were anxious to see beyond his gray squat barracks
With tin roofs and tiny windows, eager to put their hands

To work crossing other memories, planting ornamental trees.

The Red Camellia

In one of those sidewalk spiritual pamphlets picked up
for a quarter, I hear news of a bridge built

with forgiveness between two brothers estranged
for fifty years, a turning toward the other across

great policed distances, their invisible thoughts sending
one moment of release, dissolving the oldest crimes

swirling in a family's weather. "Miracles are thoughts,"
the page said, in lowercase letters, and it's when

I read on about a rare uncatalogued camellia
found blooming in a stained-glass cathedral window

made from broken liquor bottles that I remembered
how abandoned we feel in the sagging middle of a fight,

neither side willing to overcome the ten thousand
obstacles strewn between blunt oration, familiar barricades,

our words impossible to track through scorn and sarcasm,
back to the triggering event, the arguments unchanged,

and then, one of us must pause long enough to see it
or the possibility of it unfolding in that desert—

the showy red petals brighter than a lion's walk,
a loveliness freed of old alliances and judgments,

a bit of glass found and snugly beveled into place,
a thought sent out from a faraway country, undefended.

Cold Beer

for Tom McGrath

I know it's said that death can be the next form of healing,
That mustard-seed moment when the dying travel through pain,
But whatever the end is, a gate, a dream, a stony stare plucked
Beside a rose, it can't account for your ignominious mutations,
The yellow gruel dribbled through an IV, the diapers cinched
Around your waist, the plaid blanket bunched to your knees
While your blood kin squabbled over stocks and bonds no one
Knew you pinched between the pages of Marx, Hegel,
And the rhyming Elizabethans. You wanted death to come
Like *revolución*, down from the mountains of a fever,
A celebration erupting in the town square, something desired,
If not entirely romantic. I held you for a moment, turned to
        leave

The clutter of mechanical fury which kept you alive,
Then you awoke, startled from your perch, the old tom cat,
No longer bleeding, undernourished, your smile unfolding
As if from a long nap. You pointed to the sagging food bags,
The plastic tubing leading to your stomach, asked if I cared
To taste the delicious pear tart and cream. You struggled to rise
Out of papery bones like a moth fluttering up through spears
Of wet morning grass, the light igniting your face, your eyes
Ready to mix argument, memory, analysis, into this impossible
Foreign moment when you've not yet arrived at the next
        unglimpsed,
Unexpected station, stuck in a joke, you said, without a ticket,
And for pity's sake did I smuggle into this joint any cold beer.

The Drunken Poet Holds Court

Like the car chase or the last-minute Hollywood shootout,
We thought the need for continual libation was over.
What outrage could he possibly unleash? What crime
Had we not already seen masked as generosity and wit?
But like last time, the whiskey swept him up effusively
And the images flew off his tongue, daring us, word
By dream, to match him. No one took the bait except
One student who slipped off her heels and rubbed her

Painted nails against his leg. She, we, all of us seduced him
With his own obsession: to invent the most beautiful phrase
That doesn't yet exist, to dissolve in its gathered body,
To curl up with it, go falling down blind into its triumph.
In the bloated face and narrow, ancient, bloodshot eyes
We had found what we wanted: the wide rim of the dangerous
World, cities on fire, knots of gold braid, the omnipotent
Gloomy fortress where we would never take up residence.

The Effigy of John Donne

St. Paul's Cathedral, London

Who can say what sound brought him to this dome,
its daily bread and wine, two worlds speeding
across his tongue—the black-throated warbler
teasing him into the vines outside his chambers,
the sky drawing his gaze east to the gold streets
common as coal dust. I listen for his angel
blowing new moons from her trumpet, the unmerited
assemblies fixed with a music sent out as a sign.

During his last illness, when the pulse clung
to a whisper, he ordered his shroud, posed
like the only son of this world and the next.
Eyes half opened, half closed, he would leave
his statue with a faint smile, a lover's doze.
As preacher he drew crowds, as poet he marveled
alone at a woman's bracelet bringing her bones
light and shining to his arms. "Lean down

my lovely angel, let me hear you circling
over my skin." How could he begin a sermon
with a kiss, not one but many strung together
like warbled notes, the body pulling down its spirit
to roam, huge and preposterous, upon the earth.
See him there. That studied face and squint cut
into alabaster. It reaches past pulpits, dresses,
and the hands of visitors who never tire of rubbing

a smudge of ashes, etched by London's great fire.

Evening with a Hungarian Poet

for Otto Orban

Your eyes came out of hiding
With talk of Budapest.
A poor man's Paris you called it—
Rivers, bridges, unmapped side streets,
Open windows in winter,
Unreachable sheets of laundry,
And complicated jokes racing
The length of the city in one day.
You said you were already old at nine,
A gargoyle gone underground,
A whole life spied in two months of siege,
While the Nazis and Russians shot dice
To become the keeper of a black gypsy dress.
You, scampering through catacombs
Like an ant lion feeding on crumbs
Fallen through floorboards,
One more little courier, as you put it,
From an afternoon of world conquest.
Memory pinched from pockets,
The mouth snarled, a laughter braved
From crawling a thousand rat-hole passageways—
These were your tools for digging
Out from that crisscrossed rubble.
What's gone with the rifle butt cracked
Against your father's head
Comes back for a different night sweat:
A barely audible knuckling along the rafters,
A half-remembered poem hauled up
From the unlit cellars of your city.

Reading Tu Fu, 1244 Years after He Failed to Secure an Official Scholar's Post

I once believed the Chinese poets had no destination,
wandering calligraphers in love with peach blossoms
and the potions of immortality, at home in the moment
like a frog in a duckweed pond. But take, for example,
Tu Fu and his family after he failed to win a post.
Invasions threw him into motion, turning his gaze
toward the wounded, war banners, watering holes
for the army's swayback horses, the countryside
stripped of firewood. What else could he do, cut off
from the sailing moon and the news from the south
but "write in the air," the unwritten histories?

Had he found himself in the imperial gardens, festooned
with silks, drunk on Li Po's wine, he might never
have slept in a hut blown apart by wind or seen
loyal citizens handed over to the wasp and scorpion.
Lost to the glitter years, he would have found safety
for his family, written of nightingales and roses.
As it was, out there, homesick, waiting for letters
to reach him, his lantern caught the faces of men
stranded on the road, fathers like himself, tired of war,
the high cost of rice, yet ready to walk old river snow,
to gather straw, scraps of wood, the many abandoned swords.

Living among Women

Skyros, Greece

Here, retired sea captains and fishermen
gather at the harbor's mouth,
nodding over gritty coffee, half-remembering
water spouts, sea nymphs, wars to the south.

Younger men pound octopus and calamari
against shoreline rocks, repair nets,
or lead burros up white stone steps
with fresh bread for the rich Athenians.

At my table the women are mostly German
or Dutch, and they've come on hydrofoils
to seek out Virgin icons, copper plates,
ruby crosses, and the slender Greek boy.

Here, too, a bronze statue, the poet Rupert Brooke,
strikes a young Apollo pose.
He never reached the Dardanelles.
Blood poisoning aboard ship flowed

through him on St. George's Day.
Buried at night by torchlight
in an olive grove, he predicted death's
"foreign corner," where he'd fight

for England, reach farther than the white
and pinkish marble cliffs of Skyros
glimpsed from a dimming porthole.
Achilles, it's said, also came ashore

to this corner, draped in his mother's scarves.
As Sparta armed the fleet for Troy,
he slipped as a girl among women
until Ulysses arrived, already the toy

of betrayed kings, a traveling salesman.
He buried armor among the ornaments,
caught Achilles eyeing the corselet
and greaves. The rest of the epic

leads to a running chariot and a hero
dragged in a circle by his heels.
The ready passions of Brooke and Achilles
dwindle from myth over ouzo and cheese:

Wine, bolts of cloth, rocky beaches
take their names, and their brave deeds
wander in the refrains of the Aegean.
But I see a moment when two men unweave

their fates, step back from battlefields.
They mingle with children, household pets,
crawl through a tunnel of arms more tingling
than the feather on a golden helmet.

The year the Great War broke loose,
Brooke journeyed to the Pacific Islands,
lived among women clustered around
green lagoons, fished the tide lines.

And Achilles, imagine, listened
to his mother's counsel, wore blue satin,
dabbled in paint, dance, Turkish perfume.
He too laughed in the company of women,

saw the Aegean bright as fired pottery,
more true than the spokes of his shield.
Both men turned, swayed back from legend,
chose the long inglorious field

of living at home, and in due time, dying.

My Old Sailors on the Graveyard Watch

There they are beside the climbing blue flowers,
Leaning on the seawall, their chins tucked
Beneath the warmth of collars. It's as though they still
Hear the ship's bells working the round of hours,
Telling them to rise and take their turn at the wheel
Or inspect the shackles, thimbles, storm sails,
Sewing palms, mooring lines, marlin spikes, and flares.
One whiskered man talks of Havana, a memory of a girl,
Paid for and given up before she unhooked her dress.
But why, another asks, drawn to the narrow alley
Threading the wharf to a blue door and the ash
Of an undulating cigar. A foghorn strokes. A light west
Rain slants the harbor's mouth as each remembers
And forgets a woman who broke the wind's pull.
Midnight: the heavens low-slung with doubt and signs.
And so they savor the salt while buoys stab
The dark and the moon turns from straw to ivory, its path
Paying out like so much unsecured, sun-bleached line.

On a Day like This

You couldn't tell potholes from dappled shade
And the thunder stayed just outside the wind's reach.
Every fifth step touched us with a drop of rain.
Light then dark swatches revealed a root depth
Of greater dark as if the sky and earth suffused.
On a day like this, something took shape that was not
Quite formed, yet near at hand, poised to take us in
As we argued about moving, packing up, finding
Another town more sweetly ready to win our luck
With a view of the sea. *Ah! for man's wild heart*
No home is possible and so we walked on, aiming
To cross the threshold beyond the yearned-for language
Of another life, beyond that enveloping twilight
Where the air and space quivered with coming storm.
We might have gone back, but it seemed as if
We had just entered the ventricle of a dream where
The shortest path through was the longest one out.
For the sake of awakening, we walked on, believing
We would finally see where we belonged, where the new
Home would stand, where the door would swing open
And the surf would beat back the years unredeemed.

PART 4

The Bomb

Remember this, he said, *Artists express conflicts.*
They don't resolve them. And for years, I lived
My life in the spirit of that college lit-class dictum,
Seeking out conflicts that haunt, confuse, and require
Sleeplessness to pursue with any strength.
Then, the branching of the road, and I had
To decide if it was worth sacrificing a paycheck
For the imagined artistic life that lay unclaimed
Before me like a continent dragged off the map.
Feed or play the fool, I said to myself, nursing
The tug between acquiescence and rebellion
As if I really were living some kind of titan epic
That eventually would be filmed for posterity.
It's when I starting lunching with this art director
At a mail-order company where I wrote copy
In between scribbled poems. Over time, I learned
He and his twin, both artists, had defused bombs in France.
Inside tunnels, beneath bridges, underneath floors,
The two brothers faced off, and in that feathery code
Twins know without a twitch, they made a name
For themselves that brought them champagne,
Caviar, and long strings of green and red grapes.
We tricked death without a whisper, he said.
Twenty years later, I thought of him crouched
Over a bomb, needling the casings open, cutting
Wires, fuses, gingerly pulling out the bomb's heart,
When I read in the paper his only son had died.
The recent live-forever cocktail of AIDS drugs
Had not defused the disease. And I can imagine
Once again, my friend entered the darkness of blood
And soil with his tool bag, thinking he could do it.

He could save his son with a trick, heal the breach,
Resolve the conflict, become again the painter
Who would make the night bend back for the day.
Not for art's sake, not for his own paltry recognition,
But for life, that cool breeze blowing through a window,
Turning the pages of a foolish-dearly child's book.

121 Waverly Place

By August the air draws down like cracked gray paint
or a collapsed tent, and nothing rises through heat
but bus fumes and the penny whistle sirens
shooting up the avenues, but in May the wisteria
can't be stopped, especially at 121 Waverly Place.
It's not as old as the scaly horizontal branches of
the hanging elm looming in Washington Square,
but old enough to have seen Poe, Millay, and Cummings
carried off. Like those poets, this unkillable ghost

vine wrestles with anything it comes in contact with,
pulls it from its fastenings, a bad neighbor for shutters,
downspouts, mortar, shingles, air conditioners, windows.
In this flash of sun, it reaches up by trailing runners,
and clawlike, embracing tendrils, tussling, crowding
out all other growth, dense clusters swaying
sinuously in the slightest breeze, what Colette called
that "flourishing, irrepressible despot" gone mad
with power of the imperial metropole, driven

to search for gold, raw materials, new markets,
slaves, the quick annexations of conquered territory,
the great hanging panicles of lavender thick
with bumblebees smothered in pollen, and dizzy
from spiraling inside the rampant, spidery jungle
and the moist, unanchored spring air. One woman,
scuttling under the periwinkle brim of her hat, says
it has always been here, even her grandmother
remembers the oily scent, and how can one ignore

the weaving of bees, woody roots like lovers' arms
twisting love with hate, mixing servitude with adornment,
all that's crooked in lower branches made straight above,
all that's revealed in the higher swags, entwined
and surreptitious below, its seeds hot and poisonous.
Gazer of the disbelieved 1835 visit of Halley's Comet,
chronicler of the Civil War amputees home from dressing
stations, spectator of dithering parades, protests, brawls,
mutterings, recitations, buffoonery, poor whisperings

in the dark, you remember where we are most weak
and lacking and too often satisfied with appearances
of beauty untouched by ugliness, disease, torment.
What had the florid Henry James called himself,
the "incorrigible observer," the watcher at the window,
a child treasuring his impressions like "winter pears"
for when he must return home to his New York street
like this one, where a torn umbrella, a shoe, and a playbill
rests beside the man on a stoop with a sign propped

between his knees: "I'm HIV positive. Sick. Help. Now."
Up there, where petals mingle and loop through, cornice
and facade flow smoothly into pinkish mauve light,
one can almost imagine an artist like Nijinsky in,
say, *Le Spectre de la Rose*, simulating this irresistible
vine, practiced in concealment, conquest, revelation,
when he applied makeup that blurred his features
into insect eyebrows, rose-petal mouth, leafy ears
until there was no telling flower from man, the dancer

unscrambling the flesh, holding one minute of eternity
on his tongue, savoring the inhuman sweetness of a floral
being not yet available for consumption or abandonment.
But there can be no comparison on this unrehearsed day
as the wildly bold wisteria strangles the air, spreads,
winds to 119 Waverly Place, rising on a thermal lift,
then up it goes over the roof to scale the parapet.
Unquenchable weed, sun-seeking flower—voyeuristic,
aggressive, high-climbing, reptilian, long-lived, tapping

at upper windows for death or is it life, the contest is on.

The Black Madonna

Here you are rearing out of submersion into the airy lacework
of the mind's stone chamber. It's what you always wanted
to be: a crumbling palace for nightingales, a church keyhole
over slimy brick, a smoke-stained, gold-domed mosaic.
It's not the stifling of desires, but their discovery you accept
from the ghosts of Venetian princes—and so you sample
roasted baby squid, risotto made with cuttlefish ink, sautéed
pickled onions. Before you know it another day blinks,
transfixed between sea and sky like some tossed
iridescent coin caught in a watery pink—which must be
the color the dead see scanning back through candles left
at their headstones.
                    Turn after turn in the labyrinth, you look
for the origin of this rosy gouache, past dark Mannerist
clouds and long-whiskered seawall cats, then you see her,
the tiny black Madonna of Salute, lighting the length
of the white marbled basilica with her hammered silver
and gold orb and carmine dress, the robed child cradled
in her left arm. She almost seems like a woman you could
invent with a shabby, horsehair brush, but you could never
contain all the woundedness and purpose in her eyes,
what they know of your cravings, intrigue, envy,
and the late hour when the mud-stroked swerve of the gondolier
is the only sound heard in the side canal where you live.

Essay on Leaves

I used to love hard physical labor,
cutting and hauling wood, pouring foundations,
digging at a tangled, gummed root
that wouldn't let go under the blows
of a spudbar, even raking the fifty sacks of leaves
from my yard was work I could lean
into with some anticipation,
since it only came once a year and,
even as a suburban man, I could dive into the leaves
to inhale the rot and molds, the old world pathogens
scarred on the undersides, the dusty perfumes
carried in the leafy veins released under my weight.
I loved raking them all together,
the large finger-shaped red oak leaves,
the honey-colored and fire-engine red maples,
the half-dollar-shaped golden cottonwoods,
then watching them spill through my hands
like nuggets dug from scree.
What had fallen in this fallen world
was rising again in the late October winds
and scattering over the lawns
and driveways like bits of brightly colored rags.
After a neck injury, I finally
hired out to a young father and his four sons
who pulled up at the curb, unannounced, on a Sunday morning,
in a wobbly, rusted truck with spray-painted,
particle-board sides, a homemade suction hose attached to a fan,
and a tarp lashed on top.
The sleekly muscled father strapped
a gas-driven power blower to his back,
and once he got it growling,

he never stopped moving. Maybe he'd underbid the job,
or maybe he was falling faster than the leaves
from some unrecoverable sense of things not adding up,
but he roamed from the backyard to the front in a scowl,
berating the boys, urging them on, driving them
through their somnambulant tasks,
yanking a rake out of one boy's hands
to show him how to dig into the leaves with snap,
shouting at another to feed more leaves
into the vacuum that spit them into the tiny, dented truck.
I kept thinking a man who carried such sculpted beauty,
square chin, high cheekbones, broad shoulders,
would turn away from the sparks of his ferocious energy
to administer words of gentle command.
One look into the boys' faces
and you could tell they were nearly broken,
shattered by the long hours, the leaf dirt,
the gasoline roar of the engines,
by their father yelling over all the sound
to make sure his instructions were heard.
They looked unapproachable like runaways
I'd seen in New York on the Tenderloin between 8th and
        Columbus,
all bloodshot milkiness in the eyes,
crouched over a grate, afraid to talk.
These sons lived beyond tears and you could easily imagine
any one of them exploding in an uncontrollable bout
of rage and sorry destruction. In this father's voice,
I heard my own father scaring me when I didn't figure out
some mechanical job as fast as he did, his words
much louder than I could track,
his jagged strength shivering my frame
like a saw skidding through a knot to bite the head of a nail.
I hated his annoyed, sullen bluster while admiring his dexterity,
his skill to make things fit together with a wrench
like the diagrams showed.

The fixers of this world were *real men*, I told myself
in a rubbery sway of mesmerized fascination and choked anger.
The rest of us broke things, whined about how much repairs
        cost,
when real men figured it out themselves,
no matter how many false starts, busted knuckles.
But where had this father's life gone awry
in the speechless world of real men?
Maybe this father couldn't afford a house
for his children or the payments on his truck.
Maybe his wife was pregnant again and he resented the new
        arrival.
I was not a father, and didn't know the pressure
of all those mouths to feed, doctor bills, the endless shirts,
boots, jackets. I could never enter his pain,
nor could he imagine mine watching him drive his business
on the backs of his children who hunkered near ground
like pack animals buckled on the trail.
I wanted to say to him *maybe you should ease up*
on the crew or *you boys like some lemonade and cookies,*
something to dispel the heat of meanness that cut
the air like animal catarrh. But I said nothing
when he came to collect, nothing about the boys' bitterness
and dazed sorrow that reminded me
of my own which I used to bury
beneath the many leaves
my father and I had raked together and made ready for fire.

Apple Trees in the Black Forest

Such color crayoned against the rain.
Their thick white blossoms
cloud the connecting meadows.
Each village in tangled mist comes

with a uniformed children's choir,
and soon the summer tourists
will arrive in busloads
to attend the reenacted wedding feast

of Prince George, who, in 1475,
sashayed in costume for twenty-three days
with his bride, Hedwig.
Down the road in Bavaria,

police raids turn up helmets, gas masks, leaflets.
At night in the Alps, a swastika
scaffolded from giant logs
burns over Germany, freighted

with the 100th anniversary of the Führer's birth.
Somewhere in these twisted valleys,
my ancestors drew out the notes of their singing,
climbed high for apples.

The town's name floats away
in my grandmother's memory.
Grossman, Grossman,
I taste her name slowed in my throat.

She can no longer pinpoint the map
where her parents planted seeds.
In her Cincinnati apartment
I bite down again

on soft appled crust.
We talk of baseball and the exotic
polysyllabic names of horses
running for big stakes in Kentucky.

Here in the Black Forest,
these clean blondes I resemble
expect me to speak Deutsch,
rave about local beer and pigs' knuckles.

"What about the camps," I ask
my grotto companion. He weaves a stein
over my head, smiles, noses forward
across a stack of greasy plates.

"Talking about Kristallnacht
can still cost a politician a seat
yet an SS captain leads a new party."
In last night's dream, a melodrama breathes—

I babble about Germans to my grand *Mutter*:
"Do you think we could ever run again
as wolves upon the earth?"
She thumps the flour board,

folds her hands into the dough,
risen once into bubbly yeast, now fallen
under blows to rise, by noon,
a second time on the stove. "I suspect,"

she said, "we are far better and worse
than we know." In my host's face
swimming over me, I collect
the tastes of her favorite *kuchen*,

watch her hands rounding the pans
with butter. Where smoke clusters
under lamps, I can't assemble the words
of a toast in a language swollen

inside my mouth. His sharp guttural
vowels race against my hesitation.
Tomorrow, it seems, I'm invited
to a country wedding where revelers,

he tells me, will plant apple seeds
for the lucky pair. There, one day
in flushed, compliant April, I can see
an old woman standing in dark fat loam,

who will smell blossoms falling near
the forest's edge, and in that falling
begin to smell the dusted cinnamon
gathered on the strudel, the sweet slices

of apple, small enough to fit a baby's tongue.

On the Night Train to Nizhni

If famine had not swept the gray plain of the Volga in 1921
When five million fell to typhus, typhoid, dysentery, and
    cholera,
With millions more thinned on nettle soup and ripened for
    terror
At the thumb of Papa Joe, if so many stories had not been lost,
Libraries demolished, schools burned, stores sacked, barbed wire
Strung through the unending Russian mud and roadlessness,
If the fatalistic immensity of a country raised on garlic slivers
And blood had not swamped so many river villages swaying
On shallow crests of mist and left mountains of rusting
    machinery,
Sagging fenceposts, potato peelings, and frayed coat sleeves,

We would not be berthed on a slow-breathing train to Nizhni,
Nursing a pot of black tea, peering into the Russian night
As if it were a threadbare cassock unfit for a baby's form,
Wounded by hope, kindled by fear, sleepless to find one girl
In an orphanage in a blue babushka, whose photo we clutch
Like an icon lit in the window of a one-flap wallet, one girl
Who would travel with us on this train, beneath a sky
Big as Jehovah, back to another world, another history
On another river sliding south to the sea long before
All these divisions and reunions made the steel wheels turn.

Lady Franklin Writes to Her Husband
15 Years Gone into the Ice

If it's true we lead two lives, through the mind
describing what the body must break down and endure,
then yes, I've hobbled cold toward the bones
of his shadow, embraced an intricate fracture.
Once I wanted our names staked at the earthly poles.
And why not, John Franklin? History swung open
like a glimmer-swathe for a few souls to scribe.
Better to plot an ice-choked route through Baffin Bay
than rule together a penal colony in Tasmania.
Seven years there with red flies in our teeth.
Nothing to feed the meridian of your third voyage
to cut the marble out of the Northwest Passage.
Swallowed by dust, you caught in the mirror a face

too freighted for command, until I swaggered up
to the Sea Lords, squared you with a mapmaker's sketch,
the most hours logged in the undissolved arctic chain.
Remember that day when his *Terror* and *Erebus*—
iron-sheathed, bluff-bowed—weighed anchor,
the best-fitted ships ever heeled for victory.
I, and all of England, never once thought
he might not round the Horn with a bolt of silk
and a tale for all time thawed from tangled rope.
As the last ship of my commission sails tomorrow,
I've come to this letter scribbled from straight lines
of a nervous palm. You are nowhere I can name,
and I am strapped to the helm of a ghost ship,

unlikely proof that marriage was conceived
for partners even in absence. Here, my words harden.
A flat whiteness blinds. My arms quiver and float
under two sweaters when I hold you near dawn,
our prized, in-between time. From pages marked
with blue, I've stared into the same colors
setting you adrift at the top of the earth.
Jolted awake, I see straggling sledge men,
the sharp spicula of driven snow puffing their faces,
scarred by fist blows, their frostbitten skin
peeled off in black flakes, large as halfpence.
John, when did the ice pack start to close?
How many winters did you prove death wrong?

If I could bring you back to this warmed sphere,
I would forego my praise of the snow's diamond walls,
their smooth interior glinting with the saddle
of heaven. I never wanted the sudden falling fog,
the rattled, unsavory ghost you've become,
your fate invisible to my pen, the truth of who we are
together, after all these failed climes, untested.
Help me, if you are there, in some airy shape
beyond my ken, to make of my days a home.
So much of what remains jangles like the macabre
invention of the ego, a jewelry slipped from the wrist.
If you can, decipher these faraway words
brandied on my tongue—*whalefish, muluk, eskimo.*

To the Black Sailor in Winslow Homer's
Gulf Stream

Between sharks, waterspouts, and snarled waves,
You pitch in a smack boat sloop, rudderless,
Mast and bowsprit broken, deserted by a schooner.
Moments from now, a rogue wave may swamp
The transom, capsize your *Anne of Key West*,
Marry your blood with the almost-human monster.
Yet you rest on one elbow, tracking toward
The whir of flying fish that could feed you.
You have faced before the split sapphire,
Survived shards, set out again with fish pots,
Water barrels, conch shells, up the Florida Straits,
Across the blue green of the Gulf to the grouper-rich
Shallows of the Little Bahama Bank.

What crossing didn't hold its wind shifts,
Its swirling sargassum eddy, its one frayed knot
Between you and the rising dorsal fin?
In the pitch of so much boil, sunlight stalls
On your chest. Hell has already spun the rigging.
Now, your sloop of weathered brown bobs,
Lightened by black while behind you a cobalt
Wave darkens the white tongue of a reef.
In this world strapped to primary colors,
A rope trails over the bow into pastel blue,
Somehow pulling you away from the tempest-white
Weaving of teeth, guiding you back into the Stream—
No slave to the storm or the dream of heaven.

After Reading Jeffers's *Original Sin*

for JH

Here, on Jeffers's ragged coast of high-running swells,
The blue mist runs so cool and tender against the shore,
You might think history had dissolved our belief in sin
And buried our hunger for more prey. What is there
To plunder inside this chain of headlands where we
Nibble, snooze, and pick berries the size of thumbs?
What does revenge matter to the gray-green quince,
Chestnut, blood-red plum my daughter passed along
The flicker's trail?

                What if Jeffers and the millenniums
Had it wrong and sin was not our first inheritance?
What if splendor like this is where we started,
The eternal echo of salt inside stone reminding us
There was nothing to pay for, nothing to be redeemed,
No depths of contrition to reach through bitter tears
And the scorn-blinded paralysis of stolen memories?
If we had rough-hewn a different stone at first light
Would our story have been written with less blood
And more ink as blue as the wave where one girl runs?

Bell Tower in Santorini

Against frost-blown arches,
The blue dome of the tower
Flares like grape hyacinth
In snow. A mottled goat
Browses the rock thistle,
Lending its cud to the threshing

Of sea combs below.
One could die here
Inside the tint of this dome
And wonder if death had passed
Or only the overlapping brush strokes
Of dream and bright wave

Rubbed smooth by salt air
And the wind from Africa.
Decoration or distillation,
This tower? Where light pours in
From crystal, this blue sphere
Invents the curvature of the earth

And nearly contains it. But what
Of heaven? Cut with the scars
Of old ragged storms,
This island, this volcanic turtle,
This Atlantis, should know how
To steer the light-torn

Passages to such a place.
Until then, that day of lava-
Swallowing color, that judgment,
We rest here while sirocco
Stirs olive branches
Draped on the seawall.

We see a squat fig tree
Nestled in scarp and remember
Black cherries in our bag.
We eat of the fruit. We sit
With the rock and sky. We listen
To bells at the rim of the world.

Russian Daughter

Here you are, finally, after all our waiting—
daughter of the Volga and Oka Rivers,
where the waters flame coppery dust
at sunset and light the trees upon the bluffs
where once the Nizhni-Novgorod fair
blended all the dialects of Russia and Asia—
Chinese in skullcaps with pigtails,
mustached Turks in fezzes, shaven-headed Kalmuks,
Armenians, Poles, Circassians, Tartars, Jews.
Standing at the Volga's edge, the fragments
of many alphabets glisten while men drink
salted tea from rusted jam-jar samovars
and crimp the corners of black bread
as if folding back the pages of a Bible.
Small as you are, you are many, gathered
at the confluence—light chestnut hair,
hazel eyes, thick-built, slow-smile, round
Slavic face, a hint of olive in your skin.

You were born beside the slow strength
of rivers and the memory of rustling silks
and wooden chests packed with pigs' hearts,
Siberian blue fox, and Persian cashmere.
You traveled a great distance even before you started
and weathered a century of disappearing
trains. Still, the Russian women
glide in step with invisible felicities,
hold many jobs, and come home
to iron, stitch, cook, soak, and pray.
No death will stop a gilded icon's breathing,
they seem to say with their eyes when
they help us take your visa photo.
Pale, shivering traveler—go ahead,
cry, squirm, shake your fist at the box camera.
You already know that inside each tear
is a globe, crisscrossed with rivers
running muddy and golden to the sea.

The Palette of Eternity

Our Russian daughter forgets herself in the running down
Of the retreating wave,
The scamper back before the next arrives—
So much blue steel Atlantic softly hammering at her feet.
And though the memory of this century swirls
Somewhere back in her blood,
She's not looking
Past the shrimp boats boom-rocking offshore
To the million miles of barbed wire rusting
In the country of her birth.
What was that dark slashing fury all about?
Who can fathom the cost of so much craving
In the midst of undiminished icon faith?
Will she ever want to ask?
Of this day, her pulse beats in the purple whelk's throat.
Every plankton cell salts through her
In a generous splash scattering.
As an eight-member string of pelicans weaves in and out
Of one low curling wave,
I keep thinking it must snap apart from hunger, fatigue, or
     boredom,
But it holds and glides on until it vanishes
Like a curlicue of smoke.
The desire to destroy and the desire to possess
Can't reach her yet.
Which is why my 80–year-old mother paints this scene.
To freeze, even in this scorching June heat,
This hovering on the periphery of one girl's future.
Not of her blood. Not of her history. But eternal just the same.

The Answer Seemed Imminent

We heard the ship's bell all the way from shore.
The rumbling of her engines mingled with the gusts,
And the wind mixed with the squeaking of coquina
Beneath our feet. She was headed out into rough seas,
Just south of east, leaning into it, a cold rain raking
Her decks. Nothing about this departure struck us
As comforting, yet the way she stood up under weather,
The way she ironed out the crests, the way she extravagantly
Left us watching behind a veil of rain, made us reconsider
The meaning of her bell. This was no signal of trouble,
We decided, but a bold promise that the long-awaited answer
To the sorrows of the faraway world would return
From her echo sinking into the hard-running thunder.
We had given so much to her. She had given more.
Like last time, she'd be gone for years and we'd forget
We'd ever seen the sheer of her transom, but now,
Before the next squalls rushed in from the naked west,
Was a time of long listening, the answer seemed imminent.

Illinois Poetry Series
Laurence Lieberman, Editor

The Passion of the Right-Angled Man
  T. R. Hummer (1984)

Dear John, Dear Coltrane
  Michael S. Harper (1985)

Poems from the Sangamon
  John Knoepfle (1985)

In It
  Stephen Berg (1986)

The Ghosts of Who We Were
  Phyllis Thompson (1986)

Moon in a Mason Jar
  Robert Wrigley (1986)

Lower-Class Heresy
  T. R. Hummer (1987)

Poems: New and Selected
  Frederick Morgan (1987)

Furnace Harbor: A Rhapsody of the North Country
  Philip D. Church (1988)

Bad Girl, with Hawk
  Nance Van Winckel (1988)

Blue Tango
  Michael Van Walleghen (1989)

Eden
  Dennis Schmitz (1989)

Waiting for Poppa at the Smithtown Diner
  Peter Serchuk (1990)

Great Blue
  Brendan Galvin (1990)

What My Father Believed
  Robert Wrigley (1991)

Something Grazes Our Hair
  S. J. Marks (1991)

Walking the Blind Dog
  G. E. Murray (1992)

The Sawdust War
  Jim Barnes (1992)

The God of Indeterminacy
  Sandra McPherson (1993)

Off-Season at the Edge of the World
  Debora Greger (1994)

Counting the Black Angels
  Len Roberts (1994)

Oblivion
  Stephen Berg (1995)

To Us, All Flowers Are Roses
  Lorna Goodison (1995)

Honorable Amendments
  Michael S. Harper (1995)

Points of Departure
  Miller Williams (1995)

Dance Script with Electric Ballerina
  Alice Fulton (reissue, 1996)

To the Bone: New and Selected Poems
  Sydney Lea (1996)

Floating on Solitude
  Dave Smith (3–volume reissue, 1996)

Bruised Paradise
  Kevin Stein (1996)

Walt Whitman Bathing
  David Wagoner (1996)

Rough Cut
  Thomas Swiss (1997)

Paris
  Jim Barnes (1997)

The Ways We Touch
  Miller Williams (1997)

The Rooster Mask
  Henry Hart (1998)

The Trouble-Making Finch
  Len Roberts (1998)

Grazing
  Ira Sadoff (1998)

Turn Thanks
  Lorna Goodison (1999)

Traveling Light:
Collected and New Poems
  David Wagoner (1999)

Some Jazz a While:
Collected Poems
  Miller Williams (1999)

The Iron City
  John Bensko (2000)

Songlines in Michaeltree:
New and Collected Poems
  Michael S. Harper (2000)

Pursuit of a Wound
  Sydney Lea (2000)

The Pebble: Old and New
Poems
  Mairi MacInnes (2000)

Chance Ransom
  Kevin Stein (2000)

House of Poured-Out Waters
  Jane Mead (2001)

The Silent Singer: New and
Selected Poems
  Len Roberts (2001)

The Salt Hour
  J. P. White (2001)

National Poetry Series

Eroding Witness
  Nathaniel Mackey (1985)
  Selected by Michael S. Harper

Palladium
  Alice Fulton (1986)
  Selected by Mark Strand

Cities in Motion
  Sylvia Moss (1987)
  Selected by Derek Walcott

The Hand of God and a Few
Bright Flowers
  William Olsen (1988)
  Selected by David Wagoner

The Great Bird of Love
  Paul Zimmer (1989)
  Selected by William Stafford

Stubborn
  Roland Flint (1990)
  Selected by Dave Smith

The Surface
  Laura Mullen (1991)
  Selected by C. K. Williams

The Dig
  Lynn Emanuel (1992)
  Selected by Gerald Stern

My Alexandria
  Mark Doty (1993)
  Selected by Philip Levine

The High Road to Taos
  Martin Edmunds (1994)
  Selected by Donald Hall

Theater of Animals
  Samn Stockwell (1995)
  Selected by Louise Glück

The Broken World
  Marcus Cafagña (1996)
  Selected by Yusef
  Komunyakaa

Nine Skies
  A. V. Christie (1997)
  Selected by Sandra
  McPherson

Lost Wax
  Heather Ramsdell (1998)
  Selected by James Tate

So Often the Pitcher Goes to
Water until It Breaks
  Rigoberto González (1999)
  Selected by Ai

Renunciation
  Corey Marks (2000)
  Selected by Philip Levine

Other Poetry Volumes

Local Men and *Domains*
  James Whitehead (1987)

Her Soul beneath the Bone:
Women's Poetry on Breast
Cancer
  Edited by Leatrice Lifshitz
  (1988)

Days from a Dream Almanac
  Dennis Tedlock (1990)

Working Classics: Poems on
Industrial Life
  *Edited by Peter Oresick and
  Nicholas Coles* (1990)

Hummers, Knucklers, and Slow
Curves: Contemporary Baseball
Poems
  Edited by Don Johnson (1991)

The Double Reckoning of
Christopher Columbus
  Barbara Helfgott Hyett (1992)

Selected Poems
  Jean Garrigue (1992)

New and Selected Poems,
1962–92
  Laurence Lieberman (1993)

The Dig and *Hotel Fiesta*
  Lynn Emanuel (1994)

For a Living: The Poetry
of Work
  *Edited by Nicholas Coles and
  Peter Oresick* (1995)

The Tracks We Leave: Poems
on Endangered Wildlife of
North America
  Barbara Helfgott Hyett (1996)

Peasants Wake for Fellini's
Casanova and Other Poems
  *Andrea Zanzotto; edited and
  translated by John P. Welle and
  Ruth Feldman; drawings by
  Federico Fellini and Augusto
  Murer* (1997)

Moon in a Mason Jar and *What
My Father Believed*
  Robert Wrigley (1997)

The Wild Card: Selected
Poems, Early and Late
  *Karl Shapiro; edited by Stanley
  Kunitz and David Ignatow*
  (1998)

Turtle, Swan and *Bethlehem in
Broad Daylight*
  Mark Doty (2000)

Typeset in 10.5/15 Janson
with Castellar display
Designed by Copenhaver Cumpston
Composed by Jim Proefrock
at the University of Illinois Press
Manufactured by Cushing-Malloy, Inc.

University of Illinois Press
1325 South Oak Street
Champaign, IL 61820-6903
www.press.uillinois.edu